JESUS APPRENTICE

DOING WHAT JESUS DID

Jesus Apprentice:
Doing What Jesus Did

Book
978-1-4267-8773-7
978-1-4267-9390-5 eBook

DVD
978-1-4267-8775-1

Leader Guide
978-1-4267-8777-5
978-1-63088-038-5 eBook

For more information, visit
www.AbingdonPress.com

APPRENTICE

DOING WHAT JESUS DID

JEFF KIRBY

Abingdon Press
Nashville

Jesus Apprentice:
Doing What Jesus Did

This book is printed on elemental, chlorine-free paper.
ISBN 978-1-4267-8773-7

2015 2016 2017 2018 2019 2020 2021 2022 2023 2024 — 10 9 8 7 6 5 4 3 2 1
MANUFACTURED IN THE UNITED STATES OF AMERICA

CONTENTS

To the late Richard Beach,
my spiritual father, mentor, and friend.
1 Corinthians 4:15

INTRODUCTION
THE DAY I MET JESUS

I was halfway through my junior year of high school when I got expelled for a week because of an infraction, the details of which need not concern you! A youth pastor at a local Presbyterian church had taken an interest in me, and following the painfully quiet ride home from my expulsion, I jumped out of the back seat of my parents' Pontiac and made my way to the youth pastor's house. I knocked on his door and said, "Tell me again about Jesus."

Upon hearing a brief but clear four-point gospel message, I bowed my head and fell to my knees. I told God I was sorry for how I was living and asked him to please forgive my sins and to send his Son, Jesus, to come and live in my heart. In that moment I was gloriously and convincingly converted. Heaven kissed a patch of Midwest suburban earth that day, as a stumbling, bumbling, going-nowhere high school flunky knelt down a non-Christian and stood up a Christian.

I recently celebrated the forty-third anniversary of my spiritual rebirth. Little could I have imagined that years later I would be given the supreme honor of offering that youth pastor's eulogy inside a packed Presbyterian sanctuary, just a stone's throw from the place of my personal awakening. My dear friend and spiritual mentor had finally lost his eighteen-year battle against cancer. I believe he is more alive now than I can begin to imagine.

Two new disciplines became part of my life: doing my homework and reading the Bible.

Beginning that day forty-three years ago, my life trajectory was immediately reversed. I went from all Ds and Fs to the honor roll. To my parents' amazement, two new disciplines became part of my life without any external exhortations: doing my homework and reading the Bible. Emulating my spiritual mentor, I began to teach a weekly Bible study—initially to two middle school students I picked up hitchhiking, and within a month to almost a hundred kids.

I learned to share my faith with some effectiveness and grew in confidence when praying with others to receive Christ. I even offered healing prayers for injured members of the high school football team and their families. My dear mother wrote a letter to our family members on the East Coast and said, "Well, Jeff's latest thing is to 'become a Christian.' I don't think it will last very long, but for the moment life is wonderful!" At sixteen years of age, I was beginning to discover the vocation that would be my life's work. I was in Christian ministry.

I was witness to the reality that people are being prepared by God for heartfelt conversations about the Christian faith. I had the great joy of seeing high school classmates and teachers, family members and strangers respond to the gospel. In fact, there were so many people becoming Christians that I was concerned. One day I went to ask my mentor about an issue that was becoming an increasing source of worry for me: "What are we going to do with the rest of our lives once everybody becomes a Christian?" Lovingly, he responded, "Not to worry Jeff, we have plenty of work yet to do."

Since then, I have experienced lots of ups and downs, some wonderful joy-filled seasons and some very painful ones. Through it all, though, I have never gotten over my amazement that there is a God in heaven who has set his love upon insignificant, immature, and selfish people like Jeff Kirby. That now-familiar thought still gives me chills as I write these words. God in heaven loves all of us who continue to rebel against his reign. He has come to help us and to pour out his love upon us in the person of his Spirit. That simple truth is why the message of the Christian faith is called the gospel. *Gospel* means "good news." If we can only help people see that truth for what it is, they will beat down the doors of our churches and give their lives to Jesus.

Following several years of college and seminary, I found myself the pastor of a church that had grown out of a home Bible study skillfully led by a doctor and his wife. You can imagine my dismay when I discovered the sad reality that very little of what I had studied at school had prepared me for running a church. In fact, there was not much that I could find in any of my New Testament studies about how to run a church.

I tried my best, but after some years of vocational ministry I realized that my love had grown cold. People were not responding to the gospel as I had experienced it in my youth, or perhaps I was not as excited about sharing the message as I had been. Where once I had been clear and bold in my witness, I was now guarded and less confident. I had to confess painfully to God and to myself that I had lost my way. I had exchanged my passion about sharing God's thrilling news for the boring and often depressing administrative chores of running a church. Church leadership meetings were about as pleasant as a root canal.

**My love had grown cold. Where once
I had been clear and bold in my witness,
I was now guarded and less confident.**

Many of the people attending that church shared my lethargy. Some were bogged down in problems of addiction to drink, drugs, and pornography. Others had problems with marriage, health, kids, money, and vocation. Such topics became my daily pastoral fare. Worse yet, these folks needed professional pastoral care and counsel, but I was not a trained therapist and had never wanted to be one. My parishioners and I had become victims of a cultural shift. I had been called as pastor, teacher, and evangelist, but I had become a poor man's therapist. I felt guilty that my parishioners were not receiving the kind of help they needed. I considered leaving the ministry but could not figure out where to go.

I reached a point where, like the prodigal son who came to his senses a long way from home, I needed to return to my theological home. I still believed that the gospel was powerful and true and that God possessed compassion to save, heal, and make all things new. I recommitted myself to do the things I had done at first. I sought a path to reengage with the task of evangelism and discipleship.

As part of my reawakening, I decided to focus on the content and methodology of Jesus. I kept asking myself and those I respected: What does it mean for us now, in the twenty-first century, to be disciples of Jesus? What is the essential content of the gospel, and how can we make disciples today?

As a result of these thoughts and conversations, I began to perceive a wide gap between what seems clear in the teachings and expectations of Jesus for his followers, and what life and ministry actually look like for us. I found myself thinking: What Jesus promised was the kingdom of God, but what he got was the church!

In John 14:12, Jesus said, "Very truly I tell you, whoever believes in me will do the works I have been doing." Based on that key Scripture, and in response to my growing personal dissatisfaction, I have tried to clear away the clutter of contemporary life to focus on the essentials of what Jesus taught and, more importantly, what Jesus did. I believe there's something lacking in my life and in our collective life as the body of Christ. Jesus commissioned his church to "go and make disciples of all nations" (Matthew 28:19), and so we need to be asking again and again what a disciple actually does.

I offer this book as a way of asking the question: What does it mean to be a disciple of Jesus?

CHAPTER ONE
THE MESSAGE AND METHODS OF JESUS

Listen, my son, to your father's instruction
    and do not forsake your mother's teaching.
They are a garland to grace your head
    and a chain to adorn your neck. (Proverbs 1:8-9)

CHAPTER ONE
THE MESSAGE AND METHODS OF JESUS

What did Jesus have in mind when he gathered a small cadre of followers and asked them to leave behind family, vocation, and all that was familiar and to follow him? It is clear that Jesus expected to live among his disciples in such a way that they would become like him, able to do what they saw him doing. In teaching like this, Jesus was not alone.

REPLICATING THE LIFE OF THE TEACHER

Learning in the ancient world was based on a personal relationship between a teacher and student. If you were transported back to ancient Palestine, you would witness the common sight of a rabbi (teacher) walking about followed by an attentive group of students or disciples. The Old Testament prophets, for example, had their scribes or "understudies," who were given the task of putting into written form the oracles of the prophets: "So Jeremiah called Baruch son of Neriah, and while Jeremiah dictated all the words the Lord had spoken to him, Baruch wrote them on the scroll" (Jeremiah 36:4).

The pattern of mentoring in the ancient world had a very clearly defined purpose: to replicate the life of the teacher in the student. Teaching was done orally, which of course required very close physical proximity between teacher and student. The intended outcome was the re-creation of the teacher's knowledge and skillful living within the life of the emerging leader.

Does this sound quaint and no longer relevant in the midst of texts and tweets? These amazing and constantly emerging new ways to communicate are wonderful tools to help us build personal relationships. But having a thousand "friends" on Facebook doesn't assure that you have three friends who will encourage and guide you in your faith.

The primary unit for education was (and still is) the nuclear family. Both father and mother were involved in the education of their children. This is the pattern in the Book of Exodus when God was giving instructions to the people of promise after the Passover and their exodus from Egypt. God instructed Moses to institutionalize through families the remembrance of these saving events. God knew that as the years passed, a time would come when the children would ask, "Why are we doing this? What does all this stuff mean?" The story about God's saving actions in delivering Israel from four hundred years of slavery was to be told, retold, and reenacted. In this way, Israel's redemptive story was to be remembered and memorized by each succeeding generation. (See Deuteronomy 6:20-25.)

The entire Book of Proverbs is based upon this educational pattern in families:

> *Listen, my son, to your father's instruction*
> *and do not forsake your mother's teaching.*
> *They are a garland to grace your head*
> *and a chain to adorn your neck. (Proverbs 1:8-9)*

The theme of Proverbs is how to train, disciple, and mentor the emerging generation to live life with wisdom and skill. This kind of wisdom is not just academic or intellectual but moral and practical. It is a means of transferring what the parents have learned, both by personal experience and handed-down tradition, to the next generation. The parents have bestowed not just biological life but moral and spiritual life upon their children.

This kind of wisdom is not just academic or intellectual but moral and practical.

In Proverbs 6, for example, the father points out to his son the dangers of sex outside the marriage covenant and the destructive results. The outcome of this behavior, says the loving and wise father, is the devastation of your life. In the end you are like a deer with an arrow shot through its liver and left by the side of the road to rot. The Proverbs reveal God's moral law in pithy and graphic imagery intended to warn the reader about the dangers of ignoring God's word and breaking God's law. In this way the wisdom to live with skill and integrity is passed down from one generation to the next. It is in Israel's culture of spiritual mentoring that our understanding of discipleship is formed.

Sirach, a book included in the Apocrypha, was written about two centuries before Christ. This document describes the passing down of transforming inspiration from one generation to another. The younger generation is exhorted with these words: "Stand in the company of the elders. / Who is wise? Attach yourself to such a one" (Sirach 6:34 NRSV). Students were to learn by "attaching themselves" to an older and wiser mentor. The teacher would give the lesson and offer clarifying explanations. Then the student would repeat the lesson and answer the questions. Much of the learning was memorized. This was the educational system among the rabbis, passed down from generation to generation.

The purpose of this kind of education was for the student to replicate the life of the master.

The purpose of this kind of education was for the student to replicate the life of the master: "When the father [teacher] dies he will not seem to be dead, / for he has left behind him one like himself" (Sirach 30:4 NRSV). The students were diligent in observing and copying the life skills and wisdom of their rabbi mentors, just as the rabbis were trying to understand what God was doing and then imitating it. Now that is a pretty tall order! It certainly helps us understand more clearly what the Apostle Paul had in mind when he wrote these passages:

Follow God's example, therefore, as dearly loved children and walk in the way of love, just as Christ loved us and gave himself up for us as a fragrant offering and sacrifice to God. (Ephesians 5:1-2)

You became imitators of us and of the Lord.
                                (1 Thessalonians 1:6)

Whatever you have learned or received or heard from me, or seen in me—put it into practice. And the God of peace will be with you. (Philippians 4:9)

Scholars have studied the discipleship ministry of Jesus and have discerned three phases. The first phase we could call the "come and see" or introductory phase. Using the Gospel of John as our starting point, we witness how Jesus first gathered a large group of observers. Some of his early disciples had been loyal followers of John the Baptist but then switched leaders. John the Baptist took no offense at this, since he knew it would serve the greater good.

The second phase we could call the "follow me" portion. Perhaps four to six months into his public ministry, Jesus had collected a large and faithful band of followers. It was from this group that Jesus called and commissioned the seventy-two whom he sent out on an initial preaching and healing campaign. We read about their mission in the tenth chapter of Luke's Gospel.

The third phase, involving the prayerful selection of the Twelve, might be called "come and be with me in order to become like me." The selection of the Twelve appears to have been a crucial moment in the ministry of Jesus. Jesus spent all night in prayer before making his selection: "One of those days Jesus went out to a mountainside to pray, and spent the night praying to God" (Luke 6:12). That discernment process would be determinative in the future of Jesus' messianic mission. It was essential that the right disciples be selected.

Why is it important that Jesus selected twelve disciples, not eleven or thirteen, to be his inner circle? The number twelve symbolized the twelve tribes of Israel. The twelve disciples demonstrated the radical nature of Jesus' mission, which would dramatically reconstitute historic Israel, the new people of God. It was upon Peter's confession that Jesus was the Christ, the Son of the living God, that Jesus would build his congregation, as distinct from the congregation of Moses.

One of the details that people would have observed about the Twelve was that they did not come from the rabbinic "graduate schools" of Jerusalem. They were from outside the ranks of the religious professionals, both culturally and geographically. Jesus himself was an outsider, as evidenced by Nathanael's question when he was recruited by Philip: "Can anything good come out of Nazareth?" (John 1:46 NRSV). The Twelve selected by Jesus were blue-collar craftsmen, fishermen, and tax collectors.

In his wonderful book *Transforming Discipleship*, author Greg Ogden interprets the radical nature of Jesus' selection of the Twelve as it might be understood now. In the following letter, the Jordan Management Consultation responds to Jesus' unusual class of recruits:

Dear Sir:

Thank you for submitting the resumes of the twelve men you have picked for management positions in your new organization. All of them have now taken our battery of tests; we have not only run the results through our computer, but also arranged personal interviews for each of them with our psychologist and vocational aptitude consultant.

It is the staff opinion that most of your nominees are lacking in background, education and vocational aptitude for the type of enterprise that you are undertaking. They do not have the team concept. We would recommend that you continue your search for persons of experience and managerial ability and proven capability.

Simon Peter is emotionally unstable and given to fits of temper. Andrew has absolutely no qualities of leadership. The two brothers, James and John, the sons of Zebedee, place personal interest above company loyalty. Thomas demonstrates a questioning attitude that would tend to undermine morale.

We feel it is our duty to tell you that Matthew has been blacklisted by the Greater Jerusalem Better Business Bureau. James, the son of Alphaeus, and Thaddeus definitely have radical leanings, and they both registered a high score on the manic-depressive scale.

One of the candidates, however, shows great potential. He is a man of ability and resourcefulness, meets people well, has a keen business mind and has contacts in high places. He is highly motivated, ambitious and responsible. We recommend Judas Iscariot as your controller and right-hand man. All of the other profiles are self-explanatory.

We wish you every success in your new venture.

Sincerely yours,
Jordan Management Consultants[1]

It was in this culture of spiritual replication that the historical Jesus lived. Knowing the context helps us understand the religious and educational culture of Jesus and the apostles. It also helps us understand many of the Gospel stories. If it was Jesus' intention to replicate his life and effective ministry in his followers' lives, then many of the New Testament stories make much more sense. For example, here are two contrasting stories from the Gospels.

The first story is from Matthew 17. At this point the disciples had been with Jesus some time, perhaps two years. A father came to Jesus bringing his son, who was being influenced by spiritual powers of darkness. The desperate father told Jesus, "I brought him to your disciples, but they could not heal him" (Matthew 17:16).

Jesus' response was one of total frustration. He asked the disciples, "How many times do I have to go over these things?

How much longer do I have to put up with this? Bring the boy here" (17:18 *The Message*).

If you were a disciple being mentored, I don't believe you would ever want to hear the words "How long do I have to put up with this?" It seems very clear that Jesus expected the disciples to be able to heal the boy.

In the second story, found in Luke 10, Jesus sent out seventy-two followers with these instructions: "When you enter a town and are welcomed, eat what is offered to you. Heal the sick who are there and tell them, 'The kingdom of God has come near to you'" (Luke 10:8-9). In essence, Jesus was commanding them to preach the gospel, pray for the sick, and free the people who were under the influence of spiritual darkness. Then Jesus emphasized the principle underlying those commands: "Whoever listens to you listens to me; whoever rejects you rejects me; but whoever rejects me rejects him who sent me" (10:16). In other words, these "sent ones" (*apostle* literally means "a person who is sent") were going in the role of and with the *authority* of Jesus, the one who sent them.

Upon their return, the apostles were understandably excited at their initial success. To paraphrase their exalted language, they declared: "Wow! This kingdom of God power really works! When we commanded demons to leave, they left! When we prayed for sick people, they got better!"

Hearing the apostles, Jesus responded in a very curious and mysterious way. "I saw Satan fall like lightning from heaven. I have given you authority to trample on snakes and scorpions and to overcome all the power of the enemy" (10:18-19). But then—and watch this carefully—Jesus turned to his Father in a prayer of explosive celebration, saying, "I praise you, Father, Lord of heaven and earth, because you have hidden these things from the wise and learned, and revealed them to little children. Yes, Father, for this is what you were pleased to do" (10:21).

What would cause the God of the universe in human form to be so happy at that moment? He was happy because these apprentice learners were beginning to understand their essential role in realizing God's plan to save and heal the world he loved. Jesus was thrilled that the divine plan, hidden in the private councils of heaven before the world began, was at last beginning to be revealed. The unfolding drama of human redemption had just moved closer to its climax. The little children—those without theological sophistication or pedigree, those long overlooked and undervalued—were being given the task above all tasks: to announce the breaking in of God's loving rule and reign.

Jesus' way of teaching, like that used by other rabbis of the time, was highly relational. Personal discipleship was his method. People were his program.

What Was Jesus' Central Message?

If personal discipleship was Jesus' method, what was his essential message? After all, a method without a compelling message is really just hanging out with your friends. If we study the Scriptures, we see that, even though Jesus' teaching method was not unique, the content of his message certainly was. Jesus' central message was his announcement of the kingdom of God. When Jesus preached, it was about the kingdom of God. When he taught parables, it was to illustrate the kingdom of God. When he healed the sick, it was understood to be evidence—a sign—that the kingdom of God was breaking into our human world. When Jesus cast out demons, it was proof positive that the kingdom of God was present among the people. "'The time has come,' he said. 'The kingdom of God has come near. Repent and believe the good news!'" (Mark 1:15).

A method without a compelling message is really just hanging out with your friends.

But what exactly did Jesus mean by the kingdom of God? When we think of a kingdom today, we automatically think in terms of a geographic location, such as the kingdom of Saudi Arabia or the United Kingdom. But when Jesus used the phrase, he meant the dynamic rule or reign of God, the sphere of God's influence, the realization of God's power and will in a place and time it had not been known before.

When Jesus talked about the kingdom of God, he didn't mean some far-off, ethereal hope but the specific rule and reign of God breaking into the here and now. We read in Matthew's Gospel that Jesus went throughout all of Galilee teaching in the synagogues, preaching the good news of the Kingdom, and healing the sick and oppressed. With the coming of Jesus, salvation was no longer available only in the future. It was present and available right then.

To enter this Kingdom, said Jesus, we must repent, turn the direction of our lives around, and believe. The Kingdom message is an invitation to step into the realm where God is offering the gift of righteousness and the forgiveness of sins. Entering this Kingdom involves a complete reorientation of one's life direction and goals. We are to seek first God's kingdom and righteousness, believing that all other matters of life will fall into their proper place. We should not expect this reorientation of life to be easy, immediate, or without setbacks. After all, we have been living the whole of our lives heading in one direction, in the direction of our own agendas and plans. A radical change will not be easy.

"The kingdom of God is like . . ."

The primary way that Jesus taught was by storytelling. Parables were stories that Jesus created and taught in order to communicate essential spiritual truths, especially as a means of helping his listeners understand the unexpected way that God's rule was coming to earth. Most of Jesus' parables began, "The kingdom of God is like . . . ." In his parables, Jesus redefined the coming of the Kingdom, clarifying misunderstandings that previous traditions and certain Old Testament texts had created.

One of the joys of my ministry in recent years has been to lead educational tours around Israel and into Jordan. With each group, we take a few hours to travel by wooden boat across the northern side of the Sea of Galilee. On one such journey our boat captain had turned off the motors, and we sat floating, facing north, on a perfect sun-filled morning. After our guide had spoken, he invited me to give a spontaneous message to my fifty traveling companions. At once, the passage from Matthew came to me: "Jesus went through all the towns and villages, teaching in their synagogues, proclaiming the good news of the kingdom and healing every disease and sickness" (9:35).

There, spread out before us, were illustrations of Jesus' three-part ministry. To our left sat the beautiful Mount of the Beatitudes, where it is believed Jesus preached the Sermon on the Mount. (*Jesus came preaching.*) Straight in front of us lay the historic remains of the village of Capernaum, including ruins of the synagogue where Jesus taught and the home of Peter's mother-in-law where Jesus healed. (*Jesus came teaching and healing.*) And to our right was the area we know as the region of Gerasenes, where Jesus cast out a legion of demons. (*Jesus came delivering people from darkness.*) It is little wonder that "large crowds from Galilee, the Decapolis, Jerusalem, Judea and the region across the Jordan followed him" (Matthew 4:25). Though millions of Christ followers down through the ages have not been given the gift of visiting Israel, for those who have, scenes such as this help make the stories of Jesus even more memorable and trustworthy.

WHAT IS THE CHALLENGE OF DISCIPLESHIP TODAY?

When we hear about discipleship in the church today, many different images come to mind. For some Christians, the path of discipleship is primarily academic. We study, study, and study. Personally I love this approach, as the built-in floor-to-ceiling bookcases in my home library clearly prove. We can work to master the Bible, even learning its original languages of Hebrew and Greek. We can examine our theologies. We can acquire information that includes history, philosophy, textual criticism, and form criticism. There is so much to learn, and all of it can be beneficial and exciting. Really! But the academic approach comes with a warning from Jesus himself. He told the scholars of his day that they were searching the Scriptures looking for life, but in fact the Scriptures testified about *him*. In other words, we can master the Scriptures but miss the Master.

For other Christians, discipleship is a path of spiritual disciplines or "soul training." Great help can be found here. I have been deeply and helpfully challenged by the biblical and very practical wisdom of writers and teachers such as Dallas Willard, Richard Foster, and James Bryan Smith.

Other Christians define discipleship as a path of self-denial and asceticism, bypassing earthy pleasures for spiritual gains. This path might include rigorous forms such as prolonged fasting, sexual abstinence within marriage for an agreed-upon time, spending long hours in prayer, or silent meditation. A ministry not far from where I live has been praying without pause in organized shifts since 1999.

Still other Christians encourage discipleship that comes through intensive charismatic experiences, including speaking in tongues, having visions, or the giving and receiving of prophecies. In this tradition, believers advance on the path of discipleship by a series of significant spiritual encounters and experiences.

Yet other Christians emphasize service among the poor and disadvantaged. In this very meaningful biblical tradition, believers live and serve among the little, the least, the lonely, and the lost, knowing that in doing so they serve Christ himself.

All these pathways have been part of my Christian discipleship, and all have clear biblical foundations. It must also be said, however, that none of these paths insures that disciples are being created. The same can be said, for that matter, about church programs. Our temptation in today's church is to believe that programs alone can produce disciples. Those of us who have been running programs for years realize that programs alone, while beneficial, will not make disciples. In *The Lost Art of Disciple Making*, Leroy Eims says: "Disciples cannot be mass produced. We cannot drop people into a program and see disciples emerge at the end of the production line. It takes time to make disciples. It takes individual personal attention."[2]

Discipleship is nothing less than Jesus' very life being created within each of us by the power and work of the Holy Spirit.

We are still called to make disciples today, and the best method and message of discipleship is the one Jesus gave us. Discipleship is nothing less than Jesus' very life being created within each of us by the power and work of the Holy Spirit. This kind of discipleship involves knowing, believing, and—most important—actually doing what Jesus did. As described in Luke 10, Jesus called, equipped, and empowered his apprentice disciples to do three essential things:

- Share the good news of God's kingdom
- Heal the sick and suffering
- Push back the darkness

I believe, even though our progress is sometimes halting, that when we follow Jesus' three-part teaching—as individual Christians and together as the church—we are following an authentic path of discipleship and can consider ourselves Jesus apprentices.

CHAPTER TWO
SHARE THE GOOD NEWS
OF GOD'S KINGDOM

My message and my preaching were not with wise and persuasive words, but with a demonstration of the Spirit's power, so that your faith might not rest on human wisdom, but on God's power.

(1 Corinthians 2:4-5)

CHAPTER TWO
SHARE THE GOOD NEWS
OF GOD'S KINGDOM

Jesus came to proclaim good news. He taught his disciples to share the amazing message of redemption and salvation with others. And more than two thousand years later, he still is calling us, trusting us as his apprentices, to share the good news of Jesus Christ. The one and only God of the universe has a message for the citizens of planet Earth, and his delivery system is a community of people we call the church.

God's good news was prophesied in the Old Testament and brought into realization in the New Testament. Several centuries before the coming of Jesus, the prophet Isaiah spoke to the discouraged and defeated people of Israel about a coming day of restoration and hope. This was the text for Jesus' first recorded sermon, preached at the synagogue in his hometown of Nazareth:

"The Spirit of the Lord is on me,
> *because he has anointed me*
> *to proclaim good news to the poor.*
He has sent me to proclaim freedom for
the prisoners
> *and recovery of sight for the blind,*
to set the oppressed free,
> *to proclaim the year of the Lord's favor."*
>
> *(Luke 4:18-19)*

In Jesus, this ancient text from the prophets was coming to life at that very time and place: "Today this scripture is fulfilled in your hearing" (Luke 4:21).

EVANGELISM

Evangelism is something almost every church claims as a central reason for its existence, yet very little evangelism actually takes place.

Many of our churches have worked hard to craft their central reason for being in the form of a church mission statement. Pastors and lay committees spend countless hours working and reworking phrases that seek to express the "what and why" of the church's mission.

I collect church mission statements as I travel around the United States training pastors and leaders. I know what you're thinking: Why don't you collect something more interesting, like butterflies or seashells or autographs?

I collect church mission statements because I find them fascinating. They often include very important statements about why a particular church exists. Almost all church mission statements bear two essential features. One feature is the church's role in creating, building up, and educating disciples. The other feature involves evangelism, or helping those who do not yet know Jesus Christ come to receive him. Evangelism and edification, outreach and upbuild. Why are these two features in almost every church mission statement? Because these are the two essential things Jesus has called us to do. For example, in its statement of "Beliefs and Values" (its mission statement), the church where I serve includes this purpose: "To build a Christian community where non-religious and nominally-religious people are becoming deeply committed Christians."

The easy part of a mission statement is creating it; the difficult part is to implement it! This is especially true regarding the outward-focused portion of the statement and in some ways is similar to implementing a mission statement in the business world. Business consultants, when invited in to give thoughtful guidance to a company, sometimes begin with two challenging questions:

- What is your business?
- How is business?

In countless conversations with senior pastors and church leadership committees, I have asked both of those questions. Many people I meet with can clearly state the church's purpose or business. Far fewer are comfortable discussing how their church is doing regarding evangelism, sharing the good news.

Evangelism has fallen on hard times in the North American and Western European church. Many Christian writers have expressed their discouragement regarding evangelism. It seems that one of the things Christians and non-Christians agree on is that they hate evangelism! Evangelism, at least as it is often practiced in the church today, is something many people would not do to their pets, let alone their friends.

A recent study reported that of the over three hundred thousand churches in America, well over half of them did not introduce one new person to faith in Christ. If our business is evangelism, we must confess that business is not good.

Before we think about how to reverse this trend, let's be clear about what evangelism is. One of the great documents of recent Christian history is called the Lausanne Covenant. It was drawn up and agreed upon at the International Congress on World Evangelization at Lausanne, Switzerland, which first convened in 1974 under the global reach of Dr. Billy Graham. Paragraph 4 of the covenant is titled "The Nature of Evangelism."

> To evangelize is to spread the good news that Jesus Christ died for our sins and was raised from the dead according to the Scriptures, and that as the reigning Lord he now offers the forgiveness of sins and the liberating gifts of the Spirit to all who repent and believe. Our Christian presence in the world is indispensable to evangelism, and so is that kind of dialogue whose purpose is to listen sensitively in order to understand. But evangelism itself is the proclamation of the historical, biblical Christ as Saviour and Lord, with a view to persuading people

to come to him personally and so be reconciled to God. In issuing the gospel invitation we have no liberty to conceal the cost of discipleship. Jesus still calls all who would follow him to deny themselves, take up their cross, and identify themselves with his new community. The results of evangelism include obedience to Christ, incorporation into his Church and responsible service in the world.[1]

WHAT DOES IT LOOK LIKE TO CELEBRATE GOOD NEWS?

The gospel that Jesus preached was and is extraordinary good news—indeed the best possible news—but we seldom celebrate as if we believe it to be true. When our football team wins a big game, when our son or daughter's Little League team wins the state championship, when our country's athletes win gold medals in the Olympic Games, we rush into the streets, cheering and hugging each other, greeting strangers as if they are lifelong friends. We are passionate fans. Are we passionate apprentices of Jesus?

Hanging on my office wall is a framed copy of my father's small-town Pennsylvania newspaper dated May 8, 1945. The big, bold headline reads: "End of War in Europe Officially Proclaimed." Beneath it are two smaller headlines: "Official End of War Wednesday, Says Churchill" and, on a sobering note, "Victory Costs U.S. 800,000 Casualties." Written on a faded piece of paper in a plastic name badge and tucked into a corner of the frame are the words *Lagernummer No. 200177* and *M-Stalag IIIB*. It was my father's name badge when he served twenty-eight months in a German prison camp. Both the victory and the cost of that victory are part of the story.

You've probably seen the iconic image of a sailor in Times Square sweeping a woman off her feet and kissing her. When the war was over, there was a celebration of unimaginable joy. No one had to be scolded or convinced to go out into the streets and celebrate.

Now *that* is good news!

As wonderful as that good news was, the message of the gospel is even more glorious. The God of the universe has emptied himself of all his glory and humbled himself to put on human flesh. Not only did he come to teach, heal, and cast out evil but he took upon himself the cumulative pain, guilt, and horrors of a world gone mad. As proclaimed in the words of the great hymn "And Can It Be that I Should Gain," written by Charles Wesley, "He . . . emptied himself of all but love, and bled for Adam's helpless race."[2] Jesus then defeated the power of the grave, triumphing over evil and returning to his Father, exalted, never to die again. Jesus then poured out his life-giving Spirit upon a thirsty world and continues to pour out lavishly the "living water" that alone can satisfy the human heart. Now *that* is good news!

Clearly, one of the reasons we have lost our passion for evangelism is that we have lost the gospel message that makes evangelism worth doing. Many church members and prospective church members never get to hear the real message of the glorious gospel of peace. Many churches, whether consciously or unconsciously, promote themselves by offering what is essentially sin management, or they focus on why people should join their particular church.

We Christians often are guilty of wallowing in self-pity, lamenting how unresponsive people are to the gospel today. But the gospel message, when correctly understood, has always fired up the imaginations and creative genius of Spirit-inspired people. In fact, I am convinced the vast majority of spiritually lost and malnourished Americans would run toward the gospel if they only had a clue what it was all about. The title of a book shouts at me from my pastoral library: *They Like Jesus but Not the Church.*[3]

A NEW WAY OF SPEAKING AND TEACHING

The Apostle Paul argues at great length in 1 Corinthians 12–14 that when the church meets for worship, intelligible speech (prophecy) is valued far above unintelligible speech (speaking in tongues). And the foundation beneath all our speech must be love for those who have given their time to come and listen. The same could be said about much of our contemporary preaching and, for that matter, the whole church service. Are we sure we are answering their questions? How can we begin to reclaim the lost art of personal evangelism?

I would begin with a change of vocabulary. I am done with out-of-date language such as "winning people to Christ." If we are the winners, then our converts must be the losers. No one wants to be a loser. Nor do I talk about winning "souls." People have brains, beliefs, bodies, and lots of other important parts as well. I do not see any biblical evidence that Jesus or the apostles were only on the hunt for souls. God loves people, the whole of them in all their glorious complexities. We must examine our language to be sure we are not guilty of the error of the Corinthians, who spoke in ways no one else could understand or benefit from.

QUESTIONS PEOPLE ASK

- Why is Good Friday called "good" when it's the day Jesus died?
- If God is all good and all powerful, why do bad things happen to good people?
- Can I still be a Christian if I don't believe in the virgin birth (or in x, y, z)?
- If I believe in Jesus and I pray a lot, will my father's cancer be cured?
- Sometimes people ask me if I've been saved. Saved from what?

I also believe that, impressive as mass-campaign evangelism strategies can be, the most effective means of communicating the gospel is through well-informed, intelligent, and loving disciples who are willing to enter into personal relationships. This begins when our Christ-filled lives do most of the speaking before we ever say a word. It is much, much easier for us to talk about the message of Jesus when our living patterns have created good impressions and questions. The author of First Peter put it like this: "Always be prepared to give an answer to everyone who asks you to give the reason for the hope that you have" (1 Peter 3:15). Gospel sharing begins with gospel living. None of us will get it right all the time, but how we live should generate some questions about the hope that we have. As a friend of mine was fond of saying, "It is hard to tell the good news when you are the bad news."

THE IMPORTANCE OF TRAINING

We must provide beginning, intermediate, and advanced training in evangelism to our congregations. It does us no good to make our people feel guilty and exhort them to get out there and tell others about Jesus without offering realistic, encouraging, and applicable training. Nothing is more frustrating than being told to do something and then not being given the information and tools to do it. People need to know how to address the difficult questions thinking people have about the Christian faith. Building the confidence to share the gospel effectively with others is a lifelong challenge. I've been at it over forty years now, and I feel I am just getting started.

> **Nothing is more frustrating than being told to do something and then not being given the information and tools to do it.**

We must continually offer seeker-oriented classes or learning opportunities so that church members can invite friends with confidence that the friends will feel comfortable and want to come back. One excellent seeker-oriented program is the Alpha Course. I've been an Alpha trainer for the past nineteen years, and through the program I've worked extensively to spread the gospel. I often have church leaders tell me that Alpha will not work today. I challenge them to ask the over eight thousand adults and students who have completed Alpha at our church if that is true!

Alpha has shown that, with trained apprentices over a sustained period of time, gospel sharing can and does work.

The disciples of Jesus had a three-year, twenty-four-hour-a-day intensive learning experience with the Master. In the pattern of the rabbis, Jesus was replicating his life and ministry in the lives of his closest circle of companions. So, too, we will need training to lovingly and confidently share our story of faith and life transformation.

The disciples of Jesus had a three-year, twenty-four-hour-a-day intensive learning experience with the Master.

One of my responsibilities at my church is to lead a men's Bible study group. One of my goals with this group has been to equip and inspire the men to do the three things that Jesus taught his disciples to do and that we, as Jesus apprentices, will also do: share the good news of God's kingdom, heal the sick and suffering, and push back the darkness. For several years I have taken groups of men on weeklong mission trips, usually in early summer. In 2006, following Hurricane Katrina, we made several trips to the ravaged Gulf Coast. One week we created a base camp of tents in a church parking lot in New Orleans. Following dinner one night, I announced to the crew,

ALPHA

Alpha, a practical ten-week introduction to the gospel, originated in London and has since spread around the world. Nearly 25 million people have attended Alpha, including 2 million Americans. Alpha offers a fun and welcoming atmosphere; a gracious shared meal where guests can begin friendships with others on a common spiritual quest; a thoughtful and even humorous thirty-minute talk about an essential Christian truth; and a meeting in a smaller group of twelve to fifteen participants to discuss the evening's topic without pressure. The topics progress in a thoughtful manner beginning with "Who is Jesus?" and "Why did Jesus die?" and go on to include topics such as "Why and how do we read the Bible?"

The best way to offer Alpha or an Alpha-like course is to partner with gospel-centered Christians who are equipped to bring people to the program and encourage them to invite their friends, family members, coworkers, and others. I recently attended the opening night of the Alpha Course at Holy Trinity Brompton Church in London, the birthplace of Alpha. On a cold, rainy, foggy London night I witnessed fifteen hundred people lined up down the street and around the corner waiting to come hear about Jesus. The average age was twenty-four!

"This evening we are going to the floating casino across the street. But we will not be playing the slot machines or gambling. We will ask God to lead us to people with whom we can share God's good news and will offer prayers for the sick and struggling." You could feel a wave of nervous anxiety sweep over the group.

It often takes courage to share God's good news. But what are we afraid of?

I made it clear that the activity was not mandatory, but that I was going and anyone who wanted to join me was welcome. Eventually, aided by some healthy peer pressure and a brief training session, everybody came. What unfolded over the next two hours was amazing. We divided into pairs, offered a brief prayer, and in we went. Several pairs reported meeting people who were quite open to discussing spiritual questions and concerns. Other pairs reported feeling drawn to specific people to share with. As I was exiting the casino, I walked past two of our men with their hands on the shoulders of a very large security officer with his eyes closed and tears streaming down his cheeks. He was in need of prayer for some personal issues at home. As our team excitedly walked back to the tent village, we sounded like the returning seventy-two disciples in the Gospel of Luke: "The seventy-two returned with joy and said, 'Lord, even the demons submit to us in your name'" (Luke 10:17). There is nothing like the joy that comes when you feel that you have been used by God to encourage and help others.

It often takes courage to share God's good news. But what are we afraid of? Embarrassment? Rejection? Failure? Sharing the good news requires practice, but the rewards are life-changing. It is no accident that Jesus sent his followers out in pairs. We need to encourage each other and hold each other up as we do this most important work of sharing God's good news.

How Jesus Shared the Good News

The most effective means of sharing the gospel is through meaningful and loving personal conversations. This method was demonstrated by Jesus himself in the moving narrative of Jesus' encounter with the woman at the well, recorded in John 4.

If you have a "red letter" edition of the Bible, you know that the words spoken by Jesus are in red. Before even reading the words of this particular text, you can see the pattern of the dialogue, with the black type and red type alternating in equal measure. This tells us that Jesus and the Samaritan woman are engaged in an extended conversation, each speaking as much as the other. Faith sharing involves listening as well as speaking.

The conversation between Jesus and the woman is such a good example of listening and sharing faith that I'll show it here in its entirety. First, though, we need some context. What was Jesus doing in Samaria? Why is the location an important part of the story? Why were Jews and Samaritans hostile to each other?

Now Jesus learned that the Pharisees had heard that he
was gaining and baptizing more disciples than John—
although in fact it was not Jesus who baptized, but his

disciples. So he left Judea and went back once more to Galilee.

Now he had to go through Samaria. So he came to a town in Samaria called Sychar, near the plot of ground Jacob had given to his son Joseph. Jacob's well was there, and Jesus, tired as he was from the journey, sat down by the well. It was about noon. (John 4:1-6)

Jesus "had to go through Samaria"? In the days of Jesus, Jewish people did not travel through Samaria. There was an enormous racial and religious breach between Jews and Samaritans. If a Jewish person was "down south" in Jerusalem and needed to travel to Galilee in the north, the traveler typically went around Samaria, not through it. Samaritans were considered "unclean." So Jesus was intentionally going to people and places Jews did not typically visit. He crossed religious, cultural, and ethnic barriers. He loved people wherever he found them. Jesus had a mission that was going to unfold in this place.

Why Were Jews and Samaritans Hostile to One Another?

Jews hated Samaritans even more than they hated Gentiles. A thousand years before the coming of Christ, King David expanded the borders of Israel to their widest point. Then his son Solomon took over, and things began to crumble and come apart. In the year 922 B.C. Israel divided between the north and the south. The ten tribes to the north were called Israel; the two tribes to the south were called Judah. Two hundred years later, in 722 B.C., the Assyrians came down from the north and captured the northern portion of Israel and took many of the people away as captives. After a period of time some of those people migrated back. But by then they had intermarried with other groups and were seen as half-breeds. The Jewish people in the south saw them as unfaithful and felt nothing but animosity toward them.

The Samaritans had their own form of the Jewish faith. They believed in the five books of Moses, but they didn't believe in any of the prophets. They created a kind of alternate worship space on a mountain in the southern part of Samaria, called Mount Gerizim.

Those differences resulted in a feud over the proper place to worship—on the mountain in Samaria or in Jerusalem. In the year 128 B.C., the armies of Judah fought against Samaria and actually burned their temple down. So it's not surprising that bad feelings existed between the Jews and Samaritans.

With that context in mind, let's look at the story of the woman at the well.

JESUS AND THE WOMAN AT THE WELL: AN EXTENDED CONVERSATION

Narrator: The disciples had gone into town to buy food when the Samaritan woman came to draw water.

Jesus: Will you give me a drink?

Samaritan Woman: You are a Jew, and I am a Samaritan woman. Jews do not associate with Samaritans. Why would you ask me for a drink?

Jesus: If you knew the gift of God and realized who was making the request, you would have asked and he would have given you living water.

Samaritan Woman: Sir, you have nothing to draw with, and the well is deep. Where can you get this living water? Are you greater than our father Jacob who gave us the well and drank from it himself, as did also his sons and his livestock?

Jesus: Everyone who drinks this water will be thirsty again. But whoever drinks the water I give them will never thirst. Indeed, the water I give them will become in them a spring of water welling up to eternal life.

Samaritan Woman: Sir, give me this water, so I won't get thirsty and have to keep coming here to draw water.

Jesus: Go, call your husband and come back.

Samaritan Woman: I have no husband.

Jesus: You are right when you say you have no husband. In fact, you have had five husbands in the past, and the man you now live with is not your husband.

Samaritan Woman: Sir, I can see that you are a prophet. Our fathers worshiped on this mountain, but you Jews claim that the place where we must worship is in Jerusalem.

Jesus: You Samaritans worship what you do not know; we worship what we do know, for salvation is from the Jews. But believe me, woman, a time is coming when you will worship the Father neither on this mountain nor in Jerusalem. You will worship the Father in Spirit and in truth, for that is the kind of worshiper the Father seeks. God is spirit, and his worshipers must worship in Spirit and in truth.

Samaritan Woman: I know that the Messiah, called Christ, is coming. When he comes, he will explain everything to us.

Jesus: I, the one speaking to you—I am he.

Narrator: Just then, the disciples returned and were surprised to find him talking with a woman. But no one asked, "What do you want?" or "Why are you talking with her?" Then the woman, leaving her water jar, went back to the town and said to the people, "Come see a man who told me everything I ever did. Could this be the Messiah?"

Many of the Samaritans from that town believed in Jesus because of the woman's testimony. So when the Samaritans came to Jesus they urged him to stay with them, and he stayed two days. And because of his words many more became believers. They said to the woman, "We no longer believe just because of what you said; now we have heard for ourselves, and we know that this man really is the savior of the world."

—Adapted from John 4:1-26; 39-42

WHAT WE CAN LEARN FROM THIS CONVERSATION

The disciples were shocked that Jesus had been talking with a *woman*, of all things! The gender barrier was just as significant as racial and ethnic barriers. Women were not allowed to be witnesses in court. They were in every sense second-class citizens. The rabbis at the time began their morning prayers thanking God that they were not Gentiles but Jews, that they were not slaves but free, and that they were not women but men. Yet here was the incarnate Son of God bestowing grace and dignity upon a woman. In Galatians 3, Paul tells us that in Christ there is no longer Jew or Gentile, no longer slave or free, no longer male or female. We hear the echo of the rabbis' prayers in Paul's declaration.

Not only did Jesus speak to a woman; she was a woman who had lived a sin-hardened life. Residents of her village knew she had not scored high marks on the monogamous marriage test. The woman had failed at marriage five times and was now living with a new partner. As he demonstrated many times, Jesus had "friends in low places." He crossed the sin barrier, offering fresh, life-transforming water of spiritual renewal, forgiveness, and grace. So moved was she by the kindness and intrigue of this visitor that she proclaimed to all who would listen, "He told me everything I ever did" (John 4:39).

CIRCLES OF FAITH SHARING

I want you to notice, in terms of faith sharing, how Jesus first entered the conversation with the woman at the well. He stepped across and transcended all human barriers. Then he entered into a very thoughtful, almost cagey conversation with the woman. They began on a literal level but then moved to deeper meanings.

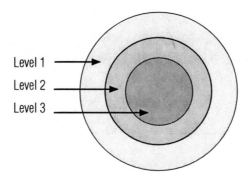

Take a card or piece of paper. Draw three circles, one inside the other: a large outer circle, then a circle inside it, and finally a small circle within that. Label the circles Levels 1, 2, 3, beginning with the outer circle and moving in. This drawing represents the three levels of interaction in human conversation.

The outer circle is where we talk about common interests. Lots of our conversations take place there, and sadly lots of them end there. Level 1 conversations might focus on a football game, a recipe, or the weather. When I lead a group, I probably have a dozen Level 1 conversations before we even begin the class.

The next circle is Level 2, where conversations take on a deeper meaning and we start talking about values, attitudes, and issues that are more important to us. These conversations are meaty and substantial, and they require thoughtfulness. An elderly family member is seriously ill. An important election is coming up. A spouse has lost her job. A child is not doing well in school.

Then there is the innermost circle, Level 3, where we engage core personal beliefs. This is the sacred ground of the soul: What is my purpose in life? Why am I here? Is it too late to change? Does God really love me?

Obviously it's important for us, especially at church, to move to Level 3. However, I think it's a mistake to move there too quickly when practicing evangelism. Perhaps someone you don't know has forced the gospel on you. It's a little bit like the old joke, in which a person goes into a movie theater and asks you, "Excuse me, is this seat saved?" and you say, "No, are you?" It's just inappropriate.

You might think of conversations that go to Level 3 too quickly as "hit-and-run evangelism." By contrast, conversations that never go beyond Level 1 are like rocks skipping along the surface of the water. Jesus struck a wonderful balance, skillfully beginning his conversation with the Samaritan woman in an appropriate way, then moving to deeper and deeper levels.

RECOGNIZING OPPORTUNITIES

I believe with all my heart that Jesus wants us to share his good news far more than we could ever imagine. One reason I am sure of this is the countless times I have found myself in conversation with someone, only to realize that the person is just waiting for the chance to talk about Jesus. It often happens to me on airplanes. I've met so many people who want to have a conversation about Jesus while I'm on a plane that some of my friends have suggested I just make it my vocation to fly! Let me share with you one such encounter.

I was invited to speak at a large church in San Diego during Holy Week. When it's late winter and you are living in Kansas City, a week in Southern California can do a person good. To make it even more appealing, my wife was able to join me for some much-needed sunshine. After a good week in San Diego, my wife and I arrived at the airport in plenty of time for our Sunday afternoon nonstop flight home, only to discover that the flight had been canceled.

"I can't figure out this Christian thing," he lamented.

The woman working the desk told us, "We can get you on a flight to Phoenix, and from there we can connect you to a Kansas City flight. But you can only make it if you run." With that, we took off for the gate. When we got there, the door for the Phoenix flight was just closing. The kind but assertive attendant let us know there were two empty seats, but they would not be together. Stepping onto the plane, we saw that the front row had an empty middle seat, but the men on both sides were so large you could barely see it! I looked at my dear wife and said, "I'm so sorry, darling, but there is your seat." I went off in search of the other empty seat.

It was located in the very back row and once again was the dreaded middle seat. I wedged my way in and sat down. As soon as the wheels were up, the man to my left opened his laptop and began to watch a movie. I couldn't help but notice he was watching the movie *Jesus of Nazareth*. After introducing myself, I asked why he had selected that movie. He responded that his family had recently relocated to the United States from Africa and that since moving here his wife had become very involved in their local Catholic church.

"I can't figure out this Christian thing," he lamented, "so I watch this movie over and over, trying to understand it."

I responded, "I've dedicated my whole life to understanding Jesus and teaching others about him. How can I help you?"

With that, we began a wonderful and energetic exploration of faith. An hour later, as we began our descent into Phoenix, he asked, "Do you believe God directed you to me today?"

"I totally believe that," I replied. "I wasn't even supposed to be on this flight."

As the plane came to a full stop he asked, "Would you please pray for me?"

I took his hand, thanked God for our chance meeting, and hurried off to meet my wife. I said to her, "Wasn't that the most wonderful flight we've ever been on?"

She looked at me as if I were insane. "Those guys drank and passed gas the entire flight. That was the worst flight ever."

To her credit, I must tell you that after hearing my story she was delighted about the little revival that had been going on in the back row. Like the early Christians, she counted her suffering worthwhile for the sake of the gospel!

RECEIVING POWER

One additional, crucial aspect of evangelism must be considered: We do it with the help of Jesus and the Holy Spirit. Jesus told the disciples, "You will receive power when the Holy Spirit comes on you; and you will be my witnesses in Jerusalem, and in all Judea and Samaria, and to the ends of the earth" (Acts 1:8). Attempting to speak the words and do the works of Jesus without his power would be like trying to compete in the Indianapolis 500 without gasoline. It just will never work, no matter how sincere the desire.

The Apostle Paul knew this truth. He reminded the Corinthian church how he had brought them the gospel.

> *When I came to you, I did not come with eloquence or human wisdom as I proclaimed to you the testimony about God. For I resolved to know nothing while I was with you except Jesus Christ and him crucified.... My message and my preaching were not with wise and persuasive words, but with a demonstration of the Spirit's power, so that your faith might not rest on human wisdom, but on God's power.*
>
> *(1 Corinthians 2:1-2, 4-5)*

In fact, so fertile was the community at Corinth for hearing and responding to the gospel that "Paul stayed in Corinth for a year and a half, teaching them the word of God" (Acts 18:11).

That is not to say that there was not great opposition to Paul's ministry in Corinth or that it was without problems and persecution. But the gospel message took root in this sin-soaked community. I have had the opportunity twice to visit the ancient ruins of Corinth. One cannot but be inspired by Paul's courageous and bold gospel declarations there.

We must not make the mistake that just because circumstances are contrary or we face some rejection, we are not right in the center of God's will. When Paul talks about a "demonstration of the Spirit's power" (1 Corinthians 2:4) he is remembering how God showed up to bear testimony that this gospel was indeed God's message. God confirmed his true message and endorsed his messengers through "signs and wonders," a New Testament pattern. This truth was affirmed in the Letter to the Hebrews:

[Our] salvation, which was first announced by the Lord, was confirmed to us by those who heard him. God also testified to it by signs, wonders and various miracles, and by gifts of the Holy Spirit distributed according to his will. (Hebrews 2:3-4)

What happened in Corinth may sound like something far beyond our experience, and for many of us it is. However, just because we have not experienced it in our churches does not make it false. We have many credible reports from around the world of God continuing to confirm the truthfulness of his gospel through signs and wonders.

On a mission trip to Haiti, I was with a team of men working to rebuild after the devastating earthquake that had left tens of thousands dead and homeless. Our team was staying an hour's drive outside Port-au-Prince, in an area of overwhelming need. One of our new Haitian friends told us that his mother at home was very ill, perhaps nearing death. A boldness came over our team, and we made plans to visit his mother the next morning at sunrise.

"My mother has improved steadily through the day."

The next morning, as roosters announced a new day, we were met by the ailing woman's son. We followed along behind him, down dirt roads and then dirt paths to a primitive home and a worsening patient. We exchanged greetings with her, read some Scripture, and offered our prayers of faith as best we could, then departed to face another day of manual labor in the heat and humidity of Haiti. As our day's work was wrapping up, we again saw the son who had greeted us in the morning. He told us, "My mother has improved steadily through the day. She is up and helping prepare the evening meal for our family." We tried to not look shocked, as if this kind of thing happened to us all the time. We thanked him for the good report and humbly offered prayers of thanksgiving to God.

Becoming Jesus apprentices is not easy. There is a stripping away of what we think we know and a deepening trust that God alone empowers us to do what he calls us to do. Christian service in God's kingdom is not a matter of what we can do, but what God can do through ordinary people like you and me. The amazing riddle of it all is why God, creator of the universe, would stoop down to place his life-giving words on the lips of very average men and women like us. This has always been his way, as Paul told the people at Corinth: "For the foolishness of God is wiser than human wisdom, and the weakness of God is stronger than human strength" (1 Corinthians 1:25).

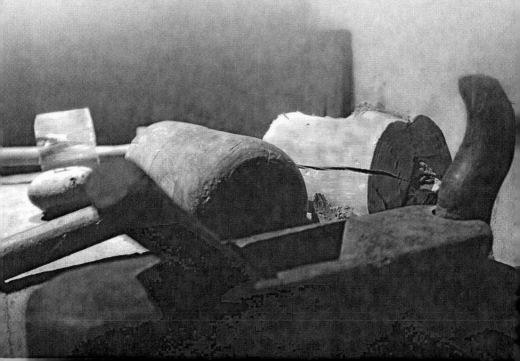

CHAPTER THREE
HEAL THE SICK AND SUFFERING

"Go back and report to John what you have seen and heard: The blind receive sight, the lame walk, those who have leprosy are cleansed, the deaf hear, the dead are raised, and the good news is proclaimed to the poor." (Luke 7:22)

CHAPTER THREE
HEAL THE SICK AND SUFFERING

Jesus Christ was the greatest healer of human malady and suffering that the world has ever known. Before looking more closely at the how and why of Jesus' healing ministry, let's take a step back and see how it fits into the larger picture.

The historic Christian belief is that Jesus shows us what God is like. The prologue of John's Gospel contains these words: "No one has ever seen God, but the one and only Son, who is himself God and is in closest relationship with the Father, has made him known" (John 1:18). Jesus makes visible what the invisible God looks like, acts like, and says to us. The Apostle Paul tells us that "the Son is the image of the invisible God, the firstborn over all creation" (Colossians 1:15).

This essential Christian understanding has far-reaching implications for us in terms of how we comprehend who God is, what he is like, and how he feels about people, especially in our suffering and loss. We sometimes mistakenly believe that when life is good and we are healthy, somehow we are responsible for this state of well-being. But when something goes wrong, disaster strikes, our health gives way, then God is to blame. Insurance companies may use the phrase "acts of God" to explain natural disasters, but that kind of thinking can seep into our feelings about all of life's negative experiences. God gets no credit for the blessings of our very existence and all of life's good fortune; but as soon as we suffer, we heap the blame on God!

As soon as we suffer, we heap the blame on God!

As Christians, how are we to understand suffering? We exist because God has willed it to be and our lives are a true gift from him. We suffer for lots of different reasons, some environmental and some the random consequences of living in a cause-and-effect world. Some of our suffering is due to our own moral failures or mismanagement of life. But we have learned from Job that suffering is not always punishment for wrongdoing. Job does nothing wrong, and yet he suffers terribly.

If it's true that Jesus has made the invisible God visible and the unseeable God observable, then our view of the world can be transformed. When bad things happen, we sometimes blame God, but if God caused those things, wouldn't we see signs of it in the life of Jesus? And yet, not once do we see Jesus walking around Galilee making healthy children sick or paralyzing people who are able to walk or causing those who can see to become blind. This observation alone should encourage us to think differently about God and his loving intentions for each human life, since each person is formed in God's image and is the object of his love. In this sense, Jesus has demonstrated in the clearest way possible God's attitude toward sickness and disease.

One might expect that a religious teacher such as Jesus would not be so interested in sick and broken bodies, but that instead he would elevate our sights to moral truths and religious principles. It is surprising, then, to see how often Jesus focuses on the physical body. Jesus' approach was not that of the Zen master who seeks to transcend or ignore the body to focus on the spirit; Jesus saw how integrated the physical is with the emotional and spiritual.

If we were to examine the Gospel of Mark, reading it as if for the first time, it would amaze us just how often Jesus is described healing the sick. Jesus was an itinerant preacher, teacher, and faith healer. A careful analysis of the four Gospels reveals that nearly one-fifth of these texts are devoted to Jesus' healing and the conversations around them. There are over forty recorded healings in the Gospels and several places where the author summarizes large numbers of healings. For example, in the Gospel of Mark we read, "The whole town gathered at the door, and Jesus healed many who had various diseases" (Mark 1:33-34).

WHY DID JESUS HEAL THE SICK AND SUFFERING?

What can we know about why Jesus healed the sick and suffering? Jesus healed people because he loved them. In Mark's account of Jesus healing a man with leprosy, we learn that, "moved with compassion, he stretched forth his hand, and touched him" (Mark 1:41 ASV). The original word for *compassion* in this translation comes from a root meaning "intestines" or "womb." Something, in other words, erupts from deep within a person. It would be like us saying something like "gets us in the gut." The compassion of Jesus is an eruption of the deepest and purest love, transformed into healing and life-giving energy. Jesus heals because he loves and acts in opposition to everything that threatens life as God intended it.

In addition to compassion, there was in Jesus' healings an element of indignation, a kind of righteous anger.

In addition to compassion, there was in Jesus' healings an element of indignation, a kind of righteous anger. This anger was not directed at the victims but at the power behind the illness. It was as if, in Jesus' eyes, the victim's body and soul were wracked by powers that did not belong there. He rebuked forces of illness such as fevers and leprosy as though they had some personal energy or existence that could be addressed. Jesus rebuked and removed forces that stole life and vibrancy from people.

It is sometimes assumed that Jesus healed in order to attract large crowds to himself. That was not his motivation. Jesus had no trouble drawing a crowd; in fact, at times crowd control was one of his biggest problems. Jesus often stayed in less populated areas so as to not create a public spectacle. Several times Jesus instructed people *not* to tell anyone they had been healed. Jesus did not heal to draw the multitudes.

The healing ministry of Jesus encompassed all manner of illnesses. He healed organic and functional disorders of the body. He healed psychic, mental, and emotional illnesses. The Gospels report that he healed fevers, blindness, deafness, paralysis, leprosy, and bleeding. Most dramatically, on three occasions he even brought the dead back to life!

Healing was something the Jewish Messiah was expected to do; that expectation was made clear in the message Jesus sent back to the imprisoned John the Baptist. When emissaries from John came asking whether Jesus was the long-expected Messiah or whether they should be looking for another, Jesus replied, "Go back and report to John what you have seen and heard: The blind receive sight, the lame walk, those who have leprosy are cleansed, the deaf hear, the dead are raised, and the good news is proclaimed to the poor" (Luke 7:22). Based on that report about Jesus' healing, John and his disciples were convinced that the Messiah had come. They knew that such healing would be a clear indication that Jesus was the Messiah, based on Isaiah 35:5-6:

> Then will the eyes of the blind be opened
> and the ears of the deaf unstopped.
> Then will the lame leap like a deer,
> and the mute tongue shout for joy.

What was the method of Jesus' healings? How did he perform healings, and what was the responsibility of those he healed? Most often Jesus healed by touch and the spoken word. There were times he healed at a distance, when a petitioner came on behalf of an ill family member or friend, and Jesus offered a word that the sick person would be made well. There were a few times Jesus applied saliva or made a mixture of water and mud, but we do not know if these held healing properties. One element that seems consistent in the healing accounts is the presence of expectation or faith. Jesus healed when faith was present. As described in the Gospel of Mark, Jesus almost appeared limited when expectations were running low and faith was weak: "He could not do any miracles there, except lay his hands on a few sick people and heal them. He was amazed at their lack of faith" (Mark 6:5-6).

Who Can Heal?

If all we had was the biblical record of what Jesus himself did, it would be fascinating but perhaps nothing more than some events that happened a long time ago in a land far away. However, the healing didn't stop with Jesus, which raises a key issue: Did Jesus expect and empower his followers, the apostles, or the early church to heal in his absence? Our answer to that question is the hinge upon which swing the doors of relevance and application for us today.

When Jesus commissioned the twelve disciples in Luke 9 and then seventy-two additional followers in Luke 10, he specifically instructed them to "heal the sick who are there and tell them, 'The kingdom of God has come near to you'" (Luke 10:9). It is clear that Jesus fully expected his followers to continue what he had been doing. Upon return from their initial mission, they exclaimed to Jesus, "Lord, even the demons submit to us in your name" (Luke 10:17). Luke adds that the seventy-two returned "with joy."

At their triumphant return, Jesus turned to God saying, "I praise you, Father, Lord of heaven and earth, because you have hidden these things from the wise and learned, and revealed them to little children. Yes, Father, for this is what you were pleased to do" (Luke 10:21).

It is important to remember that all healing power comes from God. Neither you, I, nor the seventy-two followers can heal; only God can heal. The Christian life is not about what we can do, but what God can do in and through people who make themselves wholly available to him.

The Christian life is not about what we can do, but what God can do in and through people who make themselves wholly available to him.

Here we witness Jesus at his happiest, at his most excited. Why was Jesus shouting praises to God at that moment? He must have found great joy in the realization that his followers, these simple "children," were beginning to understand and step forward into their role as messengers of the coming kingdom of God. We are so familiar with Jesus as the "man of sorrows" that it's almost surprising to think of him being so happy that he was "full of joy through the Holy Spirit" (Luke 10:21).

The Book of Acts was written by Gospel author Luke as the second half of his historical survey of what Jesus began and then continued through his people, the church. On the Day of Pentecost, fifty days after Passover when Jesus died, God sent forth his Holy Spirit to indwell and empower the new community of Jesus. The Apostle Peter passionately declared the meaning of the Spirit's outpouring as the fulfillment of the Hebrew prophets' ancient promises: "This is what was spoken by the prophet Joel: / 'In the last days, God says, / I will pour out my Spirit on all people'" (Acts 2:16-17).

On Pentecost the Holy Spirit transformed Peter from a weak and disheartened follower to a dynamic, powerful statesman for Jesus. But Peter became more than a spokesman; Jesus was now living inside Peter by the Holy Spirit, empowering him to speak and act in Jesus' place. Each of those converted and filled by the Holy Spirit on Pentecost became, in the words of C. S. Lewis, a "little Christ."[1] In those transformed lives, it is as though Jesus himself were living in and through their lives, which is of course just what Jesus had promised in the Upper Room discourse recounted in John 14–16.

Luke then recorded the first of many healing miracles performed by the followers of Jesus. Peter encountered a man crippled from birth who used to beg for alms at the gate of the Temple, and the man was healed. When people asked him about it, Peter told them, "It is Jesus' name and the faith that comes through him that has completely healed him, as you can all see" (Acts 3:16).

As the gospel of Jesus spread from Jerusalem north through Samaria, Caesarea, and into the Gentile regions of Damascus and Antioch, new messengers anointed with great power were preaching and healing the sick. Philip performed miracles in Samaria, as did Barnabas and Paul on Cyprus and in Iconium. The role of healing became a central feature of the gospel as it was announced and carried out by the apostles. The author of the Book of Hebrews tells us:

> *This salvation, which was first announced by the Lord, was confirmed to us by those who heard him. God also testified to it by signs, wonders and various miracles, and by gifts of the Holy Spirit distributed according to his will. (Hebrews 2:3-4)*

The ministry of healing in the early church was modeled by Jesus and continued by the apostles and other witnesses to the gospel message. Healing ministry was motivated by love for people, for those who suffer, and as a divine confirmation that Jesus and his messengers were endorsed by God.

When we come to the letters of Paul, we find the church had been established and was functioning as an ongoing organization, much like the synagogues scattered abroad in the Jewish Diaspora. Paul instructed the Corinthians about how spiritual gifts function dynamically, empowering the church to experience God's grace and presence in the gathered community.

> *To one there is given through the Spirit a message of wisdom, to another a message of knowledge by means of the same Spirit, to another faith by the same Spirit, to another gifts of healing by that one Spirit, to another miraculous powers, to another prophecy.*
>
> *(1 Corinthians 12:8-10a)*

According to this text, God placed within the Christian community spiritually gifted men and women who were to perform many tasks that would edify and build up the church. These gifts included healing and miraculous powers in order to give evangelistic credence to the gospel message and support to the church.

In another important New Testament text, we read that healing prayers had become part of the job description of church leaders and elders: "Is anyone among you sick? Let them call the elders of the church to pray over them and anoint them with oil in the name of the Lord. And the prayer offered in faith will make the sick person well; the Lord will raise them up" (James 5:14-15).

The healing ministry of Jesus continues today, not just as an evangelistic expression of the gospel but as part of the redemptive life of the local Christian community. And yet some churches still feel uncomfortable accepting it. There are many people who serve in roles as elders, pastors, and overseers in our church communities. I wonder how many of them have been selected because they are known for their righteous prayers.

The healing ministry of Jesus continues today as part of the redemptive life of the local Christian community.

Attitudes toward the healing ministry of Jesus and the church today seem to fall into three main categories. One group says this type of healing does not happen now and did not happen back then. The miracles were inventions by the New Testament authors or their later redactors.

A second group says that healings did happen back then, but they do not happen today. It could be, for example, that in Bible times God needed to use his mighty power, but now that the faith is well established and the Bible is written and accepted there no longer is any need for healings or miracles. This position is troubling, because it reduces healing to a temporary measure, no longer needed after the Bible was written and the church's history established.

A third group embraces healing then and now. They say, "Miracles? You want miracles? We have them every Sunday and on weeknights, too." Zealous preachers sometimes overstate their healing experiences, tarnishing what was intended by God to be a good and precious gift of grace. In some settings, exaggerated boasts and questionable techniques have reduced the church's healing ministry to manipulation of the weak and vulnerable, if not outright fraud. It's little wonder that the ministry of healing has fallen on hard times. The dilemma is captured in the title of a well-known book by C. Peter Wagner, *How to Have a Healing Ministry Without Making Your Church Sick.*[2]

RECOVERING AN AUTHENTIC BIBLICAL MINISTRY OF HEALING

Is it possible to rediscover a theology and practice of the healing ministry that avoids obvious toxic abuses and bad theology of the past? I believe it is. There are some very practical steps we can take.

It begins with a fresh stirring of the Holy Spirit. Church history reveals that whenever the church is experiencing a time of spiritual renewal and awakening, the healing ministry makes a return visit. Leaders with spiritual passion and theological clarity must step forward, laying a responsible and well-informed foundation for a ministry of healing. There is a great (and sometimes not so great) selection of books on healing, both contemporary and historical. One book I would recommend is *Healing and Christianity* by Morton Kelsey.

We must pursue a course of training in spiritual gifts in our churches. Though there has been a renewed emphasis on spiritual gifts in the past forty years, the literature has not taken us nearly far enough. A three-week seminar or twenty-question gift assessment may start the process, but more is needed. The goal is for all believers to discover, develop, and deploy their spiritual

gifts in faith and practice. A certain percentage of church members possess gifts of healing and the working of miracles, but if
they have never been trained or taught to recognize and use their
gifts, we never get to see those gifts in action.

"Now, go and pray for a thousand people, then come back and ask all your questions!"

In addition to training, we need to create opportunities for
people to learn by doing. Several years ago I enjoyed a rich
mentoring relationship with John, a man who became known
internationally for his powerful gifts of healing prayer. In the early
days of our friendship I would follow John around, watching and
listening to his every word, gesture, and Scripture quotation. I
would pester him with questions such as "Why did you say that?"
and "What inspired you to do that?"

Finally, in a moment of understandable exasperation, John
turned to me and sternly said, "Jeff, I have told you everything I
know about this. Now, go and pray for a thousand people, then
come back and ask all your questions!" His terse manner took me
back, but he was absolutely right. There is only so much we can
learn from books or even from other gifted leaders. There comes
a time when we need to step out of the boat and begin to learn
by doing.

I am often asked, "Why do you think we can learn more
about the healing ministry? Either we have that gift or we don't."
I admit there's a certain logic to the question, but when you think
about it, why should we expect spiritual gifts of healing to arrive

fully mature? I have been teaching and preaching about Jesus since I was in high school. I shudder to think what some of my early sermons and lessons were like. I trust I have made some improvement in my forty years of trying to communicate truths about Jesus. Though people identified some spiritual gifts in me as a young Christian, those gifts, like all spiritual gifts, have deepened and grown over time and will continue doing so.

A Model of Healing Prayer

Something that has helped me greatly in learning to pray for the sick and suffering is a very simple model of prayer. I believe many of us would become more comfortable praying for others if we just had a simple tool in our toolbox that would give us confidence. Let me give you a five-step model of healing prayer that has worked well for me and for others I have ministered with.

First, we determine what we are praying for, so we can make our prayers as specific as possible. I am not a doctor. I am not trying to ascertain lots of medical history or do a complete analysis of symptoms. But I need to know what I am praying for.

Second, we try to understand or discern how we are going to pray. I may ask the person to sit, or to relax and become comfortable for our prayer time. I also try to put the person at rest, not straining to conjure up great faith or to exert great emotional energy. My experience is that people need to relax, seek peace, and do the best they can to be in a place of receptivity. I always ask permission to place my hands on their shoulder or head. I am very careful not to touch people without their permission.

Third, we pray. Our prayers need to be loving, clear, and to the point. I sometimes hear prayers telling God what an awesome person we have here, reminding the God of the universe just how much this person has done for his kingdom and the church. These prayers are silly, as if God needs to be buttered up or reminded that the person is worthy of healing. Our prayers do not need to be long or drawn out. Some of Jesus' prayers for healing were quite short. Think of "Lazarus, come forth!" Now, that's quick and to the point! As we pray, we begin by inviting the Holy Spirit to come upon this person. Since the beginning of Christianity, the church has prayed, "Come, Holy Spirit." Of course, the Holy Spirit is always present, but now we are asking God to make his presence known, experienced, and felt within the person for whom we are praying.

When we pray, we do so with our eyes open.

When we pray, we do so with our eyes open. This may come naturally to some, yet be very difficult for others. There is nothing in the Bible that requires us to pray with our eyes shut. The reason for offering healing prayers with eyes open is that there is much we can learn by observing the person. For example, if we are asking the Holy Spirit to come upon someone and they have their arms wrapped tightly around themselves, they are telling us with body language that they are not very open to receiving at that time. They might be uncomfortable for many reasons, including fear, mistrust, or guilt. It may be appropriate in that situation to stop the prayer and discuss what they are feeling and how we can help them to be in a posture of receiving.

Other times when praying with eyes open, we can see that the person is having physical sensations in response to God's active presence and touch. We may observe fluttering eyelids, deep peaceful breathing, glistening perspiration, or a restful peace. Sometimes it may be difficult for the person to stand, so it's wise to provide a chair. As we gain experience, we will develop the twin skills of noticing the expressions and words of the one receiving prayer, while at the same time listening to the voice of the Holy Spirit prompting us to pray in a certain direction or to quote a biblical text.

Fourth, sometimes we may receive a "word of knowledge," which means God gives us some very specific insight or knowledge about the situation we are praying for. Sometimes these insights may come in verbal form, such as words forming on our lips as we say them aloud. Sometimes we may receive a visual image from God that we need to describe or express out loud. I have often received a brief physical sensation or pain akin to what the person receiving prayer may be experiencing.

On one occasion, we were hosting a group in our home for Bible study and friendship building. When we closed our evening in prayer, I heard God's whisper that the woman sitting across from me was experiencing very debilitating headaches. Believing it to be true but also feeling too nervous to say anything, I tried to suppress and ignore the thought. I had the same experience three times during that prayer, and each time I resisted speaking about it out loud.

At that point a brief but sharp pain shot across my head. I suspected this was the kind of pain she had been experiencing.

I flinched in guilt, realizing that I'd been thinking too much about myself, worrying that I would appear silly, and too little about her suffering. I said aloud my word of knowledge, and she looked at me with great surprise. Her eyes filled with tears and she said, "How did you know that? That's exactly what I've been experiencing for the past few weeks." Those sitting on either side of the woman prayed with hands softly resting on her shoulders. I saw her just a few evenings later, and she said her condition had improved. We don't always know the outcome of such prayer, but if God is present, the prayer will have some positive effect.

The fifth step in this simple model of prayer is to assess where we are and what else we need to be praying for. We may bring our prayer time to a close, or perhaps we have been given more insight into how we can progress. This final step may involve post-prayer encouragement and direction. Perhaps a Scripture for the person to reflect on in the coming days would be in order. Maybe some guidance is needed, such as Jesus gave to the woman who was guilty of adultery but whose sins he had so graciously forgiven. "Go now and leave your life of sin" (John 8:11) is a great bit of pastoral advice! Or maybe we decide to meet once again for a second installment of healing prayer. Establish the time, place, and direction of the next prayer session. The person should always leave the prayer time feeling loved, strengthened, and encouraged even if they have not experienced all the healing we had hoped for. I always tell those in our training sessions, "If your primary motive for healing prayer is not compassion, we will sue you for malpractice."

I want to make another point crystal clear. The ministry of healing is *never* at odds with medicine. I am crushed when I read stories of parents who withhold life-saving medicine from their children because they believe in healing rather than medicine. This is not a faith-versus-medicine issue. We are not denying the wonderful, life-giving benefits of modern medicine. When I have a headache, I ask for God's touch and relief at the same time I am reaching for the aspirin or Tylenol.

The ministry of healing is never at odds with medicine.

My oldest daughter, Jessica, is profoundly deaf. I am particularly moved by the account in Mark of a time when Jesus healed a deaf person. Jesus put his fingers in the man's ears and said, "Be opened," and suddenly the man could hear (Mark 7:32-35). I would never withhold any medical or professional help for Jessica, just as I would never withhold my prayers for her. I have had people suggest that if I had more faith, perhaps my daughter would not be deaf. That kind of comment is very hurtful. Jessica is the bravest person I have ever known. She has approached life with a selfless determination and lack of self-pity that I deeply envy. She has a measure of faith I can only hope for.

I have had pastors or lay leaders of churches tell me that God does not answer prayers for healing today. I respond by asking how many times they have offered healing prayers in the last year. "Well, to be honest, none" they may reply. We should be very careful in drawing conclusions about something we have never tried. Of course, I get discouraged when praying for others and there seems to be little or no progress. I have done many funerals of people for whom I had prayed and prayed. I have been tempted to say this is too hard for me. But, reading about Jesus and what he asked of his followers, I have concluded that I will pray as often as the opportunity presents itself, even when I feel pressed beyond my comfort zone.

Being a Jesus apprentice is not about adopting programs or attending religious services or performing helpful activities in your community, as wonderful as those things can be. Being a Jesus apprentice means having the very life of Jesus created in you and through you, by the power of the Holy Spirit. The Apostle Paul said we should continue in travail "until Christ is formed in you" (Galatians 4:19). It is God's will for us to become fully alive to the presence and power of the Holy Spirit.

Above all, we must remember that you and I cannot heal anyone. Only God can do that. The Christian life is not about what we can do, but what God can do in and through people who make themselves wholly available to him.

CHAPTER FOUR
PUSH BACK THE DARKNESS

*"Silence!" Jesus said, speaking harshly to the demon.
"Come out of him!" The unclean spirit shook him and
screamed, then it came out. (Mark 1:25-26 CEB)*

CHAPTER FOUR
PUSH BACK THE DARKNESS

How do we understand the nature and the reality of evil? It is not a subject we often talk about, and yet, if we are to become Jesus apprentices, we cannot ignore it. Jesus confronted evil again and again throughout his ministry. Understanding the biblical witness of the struggle between good and evil will help us understand what we see happening around us in the world. We will become more effective, confident apprentices of Jesus.

The mysterious cross of Christ, clouded in darkness with earthquakes and a torn Temple curtain, was the great moment of God's crushing defeat of evil. I use the word *crushing* intentionally. It's the word God uses in Genesis 3:15 to condemn the serpent in the garden of Eden ("he will crush your head"). In the unfolding drama of human redemption, God had promised to act, and Scripture records that God did exactly what he promised to do. Not that the battle is over, for life is an ongoing wrestling match, as Paul tells us: "Put on the full armor of God, so that you can take your stand against the devil's schemes" (Ephesians 6:11). But now, with the coming of Christ, the momentum has shifted and the final outcome has been assured.

We need not feel intimidated or fearful when we address the topic of evil. All through the New Testament, we find Jesus triumphing over evil.

> *Jesus and his followers went into Capernaum. Immediately on the Sabbath Jesus entered the synagogue and started teaching. The people were amazed by his teaching, for he was teaching them with authority, not like the legal experts. Suddenly, there in the synagogue, a person with an evil spirit screamed, "What have you to do with us, Jesus of Nazareth? Have you come to destroy us? I know who you are. You are the holy one from God."*
>
> *"Silence!" Jesus said, speaking harshly to the demon. "Come out of him!" The unclean spirit shook him and screamed, then it came out. (Mark 1:21-26 CEB)*

One of my favorite places in the Holy Land is the historical remains of ancient Capernaum, located on the northern coast of the Sea of Galilee. The Jewish synagogue ruins are visible, as are the foundation stones of a house where Peter's mother-in-law lived. It doesn't take much imagination to read the above passage from Mark and visualize these events taking place.

This text is commonly understood as an example of the lack of knowledge and understanding about mental illness two thousand years ago. "Back then" people blamed evil spiritual powers for anything that could not be explained in more rational ways.

But today, the logic goes, we treat mental illness like this with medication, therapy, and counseling. Case closed.

Is it really that simple, or are we glossing over something that was an essential part of Jesus' ministry and message? Let me be clear: I am not someone who finds demons around every corner or at the root of every terrible event. On the other hand, how can we see the callousness of heart and wholesale destruction of human life that are all around us and not suspect the presence of personal evil?

GOOD VERSUS EVIL IN THE BIBLE

When we draw back the curtain and observe the dramatic stories of the Bible, especially in the life of Jesus, we witness the cosmic struggle of good versus evil. The Bible doesn't give us lots of direct information about why this struggle exists or how it came to be this way, but clearly it's a central theme, because the Bible opens with Adam and Eve yielding to evil and ends with the victorious celebration of God's victory over evil.

Upon close examination of the Gospels, we discover a spiritual struggle between the forces of good and evil on almost every page. When the Magi didn't come back to tell Herod the exact time and location of the infant Messiah's birth, Herod was enraged.

> *When Herod realized that he had been outwitted by the Magi, he was furious, and he gave orders to kill all the boys in Bethlehem and its vicinity who were two years old and under, in accordance with the time he had learned from the Magi. (Matthew 2:16)*

After Jesus was baptized and anointed for public ministry, the devil struck back, attempting to destroy that ministry before it even began.

> *The devil took him to a very high mountain and showed*
> *him all the kingdoms of the world and their splendor. "All*
> *this I will give you," he said, "if you will bow down and*
> *worship me." Jesus said to him, "Away from me, Satan!*
> *For it is written: 'Worship the Lord your God, and serve*
> *him only.'" (Matthew 4:8-10)*

Judas, one of Jesus' inner circle of Twelve who served the group as treasurer, betrayed Jesus for thirty pieces of silver. Surely it was Satan who put the idea into Judas's heart to betray Jesus, and surely Satan must have delighted in the events of Golgotha.

> *Then Satan entered Judas, called Iscariot, one of the*
> *Twelve. And Judas went to the chief priests and the offi-*
> *cers of the temple guard and discussed with them how he*
> *might betray Jesus. (Luke 22:3-4)*

Finally, what appeared to be the moment of greatest darkness and the victory of evil was in fact, as explained by Paul, the beginning of its end.

> *He forgave us all our sins, having canceled the charge*
> *of our legal indebtedness, which stood against us and*
> *condemned us; he has taken it away, nailing it to the*

cross. And having disarmed the powers and authorities,
he made a public spectacle of them, triumphing over
them by the cross. (Colossians 2:13-15)

For the Christian, evil exists and it's very real. It's not an illusion. And it's here because of rebellion against God. Why study the Bible on the topic of evil? It really is an essential part of the historic Christian faith. In the last few years it has been pushed to the side, but over the centuries, understanding the defeat of evil has been an essential part of the Christian faith.

If there were demons around when Jesus was here, where have they gone, and are they still in existence?

The same people who find it impossible that Jesus ever cast out "demons" have no difficulty accepting the idea that good will overcome evil. The casting out of demons by Jesus makes complete sense when it is understood in the larger biblical narrative. In the person of Jesus, the full authority of God who is all good was recognizable to the demons who sought to kill, steal, and destroy the lives of people God created in love. Like a dark room full of cockroaches swarming the floors, when the bright light of God's rule and reign burst forth, demons ran for the corners. Their recognition of Jesus' authority was telling. Demons shrieked, "What do you want with us, Jesus of Nazareth? Have you come to destroy us? I know who you are—the Holy One of God!" (Mark 1:24).

It seems strange, and yet altogether believable, that spiritual forces would recognize who Jesus was and what he had come to do. "Have you come to destroy us?" they cried. The answer was a simple and authoritative "*Yes!*"

Perhaps part of the reason we do not often witness the shrieking of evil as it departs our churches and worship services is the low level of divine authority present among us. Millions of Christians pray every Sunday, "Deliver us from evil" (though I think a better translation is "Deliver us from the evil one"), but the words are so familiar that we often don't pay attention to what we are saying and what we are asking of God.

One of the questions I have often been asked is this: "If there were demons around when Jesus was here, where have they gone, and are they still in existence?" The answer seems to depend on who you are asking. In some traditions, casting out demons is as common as singing a hymn or taking up an offering. However, I do not believe that approach is either biblically accurate or pastorally responsible. I find it interesting that the Apostle Paul never prescribes "deliverance" from a demon as a pastoral strategy in any of his epistles, even for the guy he calls out in 1 Corinthians 5:1 for sleeping with his father's wife!

However, Paul does use the image of deliverance from the kingdom of darkness as a metaphor for the whole of Christian conversion. Paul writes, "For he has rescued us from the dominion of darkness and brought us into the kingdom of the Son he loves, in whom we have redemption, the forgiveness of sins" (Colossians 1:13-14). For the informed Christian, prayer, praise, and world-transforming service are the only reasonable responses to God for extending the gift of his love, forgiveness, indwelling Spirit, and relocation from one kingdom to another.

Though it may be true that casting out demons is not a common feature of normal Christian life, I would not dismiss altogether the fact that in extreme cases there may be spiritual powers of darkness at work. I have been present in several ministry sessions where people have been under what appeared to be spiritual oppression and demonic assault that required careful discernment and authoritative prayer. In a few rare moments, demons have spoken through their victims and challenged my ministerial calling and authority. But through the grace and power of Christ, they were silenced and sent on their way. Evidence that the experiences were real could be seen in the dramatic changes for those who experienced new life in Christ after the demons had left them.

Dr. M. Scott Peck, a distinguished physician and therapist, kept encountering something in his practice that he could not define or cure by his normal methods of counseling and prescriptions. Dr. Peck concluded that there was a small percentage of patients who suffered from what he called, for lack of a better term, "evil." Over time, empowered by his own Christian conversion and reflections, he developed a therapy that involved discerning prayer and even exorcism. In his book *People of the Lie*,[1] based on his own research, Dr. Peck reported that, based on his own experience as a therapist, the worldview and practices of Jesus were as relevant as this morning's newspaper. In addition to Dr. Peck's convincing testimony, I have learned from people I deeply respect—interestingly, more often people who are from liturgical Christian traditions—that the ministry of freeing people from spiritual powers of darkness is still a much-needed and important task.

EVIL IN CONTEMPORARY LIFE

When we talk about evil, we often remember the Holocaust. To many people, the face of Adolf Hitler represents the face of evil, the face of "the evil one" (Matthew 6:13). In winning World War II, we confronted and defeated the Nazis, but we did not forever conquer evil. Sadly, we are reminded of that hard truth every day as we read the paper and listen to the news.

For me, evil rose like a dark cloud covering the sun on July 22, 2011. It should have been a day of great joy and happiness. Earlier, my son and a Norwegian woman named Ann Marie had corresponded on the Internet for about a year, and then my son had flown to Norway to meet Ann Marie and her family in person. On that day in July, I had the privilege of officiating at my son's wedding. It was a wonderful experience, a great event, *until* ...

We found ourselves in the midst of a great darkness.

We were in the middle of the wedding rehearsal when the phone of Ann Marie's father (who is with the Norwegian police force) began to explode with messages. There had been a bombing in Oslo. We thought that was the tragedy, but it turned out to be a diversion as reports poured in through his phone of a man on an island who was shooting defenseless young people. It turned out that neighbors next door to where we were staying had two children on that island. Their daughter survived by playing dead, but their son was murdered as he tried to swim away. We found ourselves in the midst of a great darkness.

On another occasion, I sat with my friends Greg and Missy Smith through all the court proceedings of a young man who had murdered their daughter Kelsey. I had baptized Kelsey when she was nine years old, and I officiated at her funeral. It was like looking evil right in the face. The experience was a blow from which her devout and praying grandmother never recovered. I officiated at her grandmother's funeral, too.

What possesses a man to shoot innocent teenagers? What possesses a brutal tyrant to open fire on his own citizens in the Middle East? What possesses someone in the twenty-first century to behead an innocent person and record it for the world to see? We can't imagine ourselves or anyone we know perpetrating such evil acts. And yet, I am instructed by the following quote from Aleksandr Solzhenitsyn:

> If only it were all so simple! If only there were evil people somewhere insidiously committing evil deeds, and it were necessary only to separate them from the rest of us and destroy them. But the line dividing good and evil cuts through the heart of every human being. And who is willing to destroy a piece of his own heart?[2]

What Are We to Do?

I believe in personal evil. I believe that some people have been given particular spiritual gifts that enable them to cast out demons. But is there a role for every Jesus apprentice in pushing back darkness? Yes! All of us have before us a ministry of resisting or pushing back spiritual forces of darkness, through the "ordinary means" of communicating the gospel of grace.

There is a popular story about a young boy staring out the window of his grandmother's home. As dusk turned to darkness, the lamplighter coming down the street lighting the old-fashioned gas street lamps fascinated the boy. The boy called out to his grandmother, "Nana! Come quickly. There's a man coming down the street punching holes in the darkness!"

Every time the church does what Jesus instructed us to do, in word and in deed, we are punching holes in the darkness.

Every time the church does what Jesus instructed us to do, in word and in deed, we are punching holes in the darkness. In every good word spoken, every act of charity in the name of Christ, every meal served, and every prisoner visited, we are expanding the kingdom of God and reducing the kingdom of darkness.

In Chapter 2, I asked, "Are we close enough to people outside the church to be sure we are answering their questions?" In a similar way, we might ask ourselves where we see darkness in our daily lives and how we can "push back."

We see hunger, and we work in soup kitchens. We see people without a place to sleep, and we provide shelter in our church or help to build a Habitat house. We see prisoners, and we gather Christmas gifts for their children. In these ways and many others, we push back darkness.

We talked previously about sharing the good news of God's kingdom, but now I want to talk about it more specifically as a powerful way to push back darkness. A team of men and women from my church take the gospel message into local prisons. My wife, Michelle, and I had the privilege of spending all day in a maximum security prison to share the good news of the gospel as it relates to the ministry of the Holy Spirit. Teaching in a prison is always a moving and wonderful experience. We get much more out of it than we give. But I had an experience that particular day I will never forget.

I had not met that group of inmates before. Among them was a man named John who was profoundly deaf. He had the sweetest spirit about him and the sweetest countenance. But imagine this: John was in prison, and I saw no evidence that anyone there spoke sign language. So not only did he face the isolation of prison itself, separated from the rest of society, but he also faced life in prison with no one to talk to, isolated even from the other prisoners. And, as often happens with profoundly deaf adults, he could read and write at just a second- or third-grade level. Because my daughter is deaf and I can sign, I was put in the role of teaching and signing all my talks. I did the best I could to connect with John. When Michelle was teaching, I sat and tried to communicate her words in sign language. John didn't have a Bible he could read, so I gave him mine. When John smiled, I can assure you that we were pushing back the darkness.

When we share the good news in a prison, we are combating the darkness of the crime committed, the darkness of isolation, the darkness of despair. The grace of Jesus Christ is available to everyone. When we visit prisoners, we bring Light into a very dark place.

ENCOUNTERING DARKNESS IN DAILY LIFE

There are other kinds of darkness that we might not recognize in the moment, or perhaps we might recognize them but don't know what to do. Here are some examples:

> When shopping, you overhear two teenage clerks talking. They laugh about another clerk who isn't there, and they call her demeaning names. What do you do?

> Your house is being appraised in order to refinance it. In the course of the conversation, the appraiser makes a reference to "those people" who live just a few blocks away and could come to make trouble. You are bothered by the remark but really need a good appraisal on your house. What do you do?

> A family is eating in a restaurant, and one of their children has Down Syndrome. You overhear a whispered comment from someone at another table: "I feel sorry for them, but I wish they would leave. I can't enjoy my meal." Did the family hear? What do you do?

In your own life, have you ever suddenly realized that what began as a conversation of genuine concern for a friend or acquaintance has slipped over into gossip? Have you ever judged someone and then later discovered something that made you change your mind and regret your judgment? Think about the last several weeks in your life. What would you do differently, how would you think differently? Where could you have been light in the darkness?

PUSHING BACK DARKNESS WITH PRAYER

Do you sometimes feel completely overwhelmed by the darkness in the world, in our country, in your community, or in your personal life? As Jesus apprentices, we can pray with expectation and hope, however dark the world around us seems. When despair begins to overtake us, we turn to Jesus, who is the Light of the world. We have been assured that goodness will ultimately conquer evil and that the Light will conquer the darkness.

In the previous chapter on healing, you may recall that I said I would never withhold either medical help or prayer. One does not exclude the other. The same thing is true in our efforts to push back darkness. We must do everything we can in concrete, practical ways to push back against evil and darkness. This might include participating in a ministry at your church to address poverty, engaging in political efforts where changes in policies are necessary, helping someone find a much needed mental health professional. There are many, many things we can do to help those who are struggling in the dark. At the same time, we can and must pray!

Prayer is not passive. As Christians, we believe that when we pray, something happens, something changes. Of course, in many ways prayer remains a mystery, but that does not mean it is ineffective.

PRAY WHEN THE DARKNESS IS OVERWHELMING.

After the terrible events on September 11, 2001, Americans flooded into churches, including people who hadn't been in a church for years and people who never had been in a church. Why did they come? Because they wanted to honor the families who had lost a loved one. Because they were overwhelmed and afraid and didn't want to be alone in their terror.

In those moments, we didn't just want to pray; we *needed* to pray. We had experienced evil beyond our imaginations. We had previously seen evil in news reports many times, but usually it had happened *there*, not *here*. Churches were filled because suddenly a terrible evil had exploded in our midst that was too big to hold in our minds and hearts. We turned to God because only God was big enough to bear our fear and sorrow. Sometimes prayers of lament are all we can offer, but we know that God hears our prayers and is grieving with us.

PRAY WHEN THE DARKNESS AND DESPAIR INSIDE YOU OR SOMEONE YOU LOVE SEEMS TO BE WINNING.

Death of a loved one, loss of a job, addiction, depression, physical and mental illness—the darkness is never far away. It is right where you are. It is beside you, around you, even in you. Make a phone call, write a note, accept an invitation to coffee, but also pray.

PRAY FOR SOMEONE WHO IS POOR.

Pray not only for "the poor" generally but for someone you know who is poor. If you do not know a poor person by name or remembered conversation, ask God to introduce you to someone who needs many material things but also needs your prayers.

PRAY FOR PEOPLE WHO HAVE LOST HOPE.

Pray with those you know who struggle with depression and for those who have been defeated by the recurring snare of addiction and other self-defeating patterns of life.

PRAY FOR PEOPLE WHO HAVE YET TO YIELD THEIR LIVES TO THE LOVING RULE AND REIGN OF GOD.

Ask God to give you his heart of love for those who have not encountered the loving and healing embrace of God. Invite God by his Holy Spirit to give you opportunities to share what you know of his story.

VICTORY OVER EVIL

Several years ago I was attending a conference in California that had attracted a few thousand pastors and church leaders. There was a shared sense of God's presence, and many were experiencing spiritual refreshment and renewal. At one point during the proceedings, two of my pastor friends and I were summoned to a pastoral care office. Among the three of us we had years of spiritual leadership and advanced theological degrees, and one of our threesome had earned his doctorate in clinical psychology.

Upon entering the room we found a man in a state of deep distress, sitting on the floor, speaking in a deep voice not his own, uttering terrible things about Jesus. We began to offer prayers for his liberation and healing, but it quickly became clear that our prayers were availing little. A few minutes later a gentleman entered the room, a leading layperson from the host church. He was not "ordained," nor had he attended any seminary. In fact, he was the owner of a local bakery. Upon the layperson's arrival, the troubled man turned violently in his direction, and a voice shrieked, "Oh, no, not you! I know who you are." Gradually the troubled man calmed down, and in a moment he was completely at peace.

The dramatic events that took place in a Jewish synagogue on the shores of Galilee twenty centuries ago suddenly made much more sense to me.

In that brief encounter I grasped a life-transforming reality: there is authority that comes from people, from human institutions and pedigrees, and there is another type of authority that comes only from God. My ministerial friends and I had the one, and the layperson had the other. This was a humbling experience that I have never forgotten. The dramatic events that took place in a Jewish synagogue on the shores of Galilee twenty centuries ago suddenly made much more sense to me.

Of course, it's important to remember that it's not just exorcisms that are relevant here, but the whole of the Christian life that can be seen in the light of an aggressive spiritual conflagration. The Apostle Paul described the believer's daily struggle in these terms:

> *For our struggle is not against flesh and blood, but against the rulers, against the authorities, against the powers of this dark world and against the spiritual forces of evil in the heavenly realms. (Ephesians 6:12)*

To succeed in this conflict requires protective armor including a belt of truth, a breastplate of righteousness, and a shield of faith. Add to this the sword of the Spirit, that being God's word.

One aspect of Pauline theology not often mentioned in combating evil is Paul's teaching about spiritual gifts and how they function within the church, the body of Christ. In his classic text on spiritual gifts, 1 Corinthians 12–14, Paul names various gifts that serve to build up, strengthen, and encourage the community of faith. One of these gifts is "the distinguishing between spirits." According to New Testament scholar D. A. Carson, this gift functions because "there is ever a need to distinguish demonic forces from the Holy Spirit."[3]

Other New Testament writers are in full agreement with Paul. In 1 Peter 5:8 we read, "Your enemy the devil prowls around like a roaring lion looking for someone to devour." And could any text be more blunt or forceful than 1 John 3:8, which states: "The reason the Son of God appeared was to destroy the devil's works."

It is the Bible's final book, Revelation, that most powerfully describes the ultimate destruction of evil and the glorious triumph of God's own Son. In highly symbolic imagery, a woman is about to give birth to a son destined to "rule all the nations," and she is confronted by a hideous red dragon that seeks to devour the child. The vision concludes with the casting down of the dragon, the vindication of God's Messiah, and the promise that his people will overcome. These prophetic pictures assure believers that God and his kingdom will prove victorious over everything that opposes his reign. These promises give courage and hope to all believers as we face our times of trial and testing.

THE WAY FORWARD

In this study we have reflected on the message and, more particularly, the methods of Jesus. He commissioned his followers to do three things, which we as Jesus apprentices aspire to do: share the good news of God's kingdom, heal the sick and suffering, and push back the darkness. We will not do these things perfectly, and even our best seasons will be but a dim reflection of the light and life of Christ. Nevertheless we, like the original twelve disciples and those in the early church who came after, have been charged to "go and make disciple of all nations." We have been sent with authority to continue the mission that Jesus began.

We affirm that Jesus not only delivered his message but also demonstrated how best to pass it along from one generation, one group, one believer to the next. We are apprentices, and like our master we are called to make apprentices of all who are willing to follow.

Jesus' mission, and ours, does not happen in a vacuum. The gospel of God's rule and reign meets resistance at every turn. Jesus promised his apprentices that they would meet the same opposition that he faced.

> *"Whoever listens to you listens to me; whoever rejects you rejects me; but whoever rejects me rejects him who sent me." (Luke 10:16)*

What a responsibility rests upon our shoulders! Jesus has offered us the privilege and responsibility of showing the living God to a world in critical need. We hope and pray that the Lord will say of us and our churches what Paul wrote to his startup church in Thessalonica: "The Lord's message rang out from you... your faith in God has become known everywhere" (1 Thessalonians 1:8).

It's been said that vision is a clear picture of a preferable future. With that in mind, what is the way forward? What is our vision? For each of us and for the contemporary church, the way forward is a clear and consistent look at Jesus. To reach the future we long for, we must find our way back to the days of an itinerant Jewish preacher and faith healer roaming the paths of Palestine, offering a message of truth, hope, and healing. Following in his dust are those to whom he has entrusted his future enterprise: you and me.

We are important parts of the Spirit-empowered community of God who will faithfully fulfill Christ's mandate to share good news, heal the sick and suffering, and push back the powers of darkness. That's what it means to become a Jesus apprentice. I'm all in. Are you?

NOTES

Chapter One

1. http://www.servant.org/writings/parables/pa_m.php, cited in Greg Ogden, *Transforming Discipleship: Making Disciples a Few at a Time* (Downers Grove, IL: InterVarsity Press, 2003), 77.
2. Leroy Eims, *The Lost Art of Disciple Making* (Colorado Springs, CO; NavPress, 1978), 45-46.

Chapter Two

1. Jeffrey Gros (1999). "Making Christ Known: Historic Mission Documents from the Lausanne Movement, 1974–1989, edited by John Stott." *International Review of Mission* **88** (350): 313. doi:10.1111/j.1758-6631.1999.tb00161.x. See also, The Lausanne Covenant, http://www.ywam.org/about-us /lausanne-covenant/.
2. Charles Wesley, "And Can It Be that I Should Gain," *The United Methodist Hymnal* (Nashville, TN: The United Methodist Publishing House, 1989), 363, stanza 3.
3. Dan Kimball, *They Like Jesus but Not the Church: Insights from Emerging Generations* (Grand Rapids, MI: Zondervan, 2007).

Chapter Three

1. C. S. Lewis, *Mere Christianity* (New York: HarperOne, 2001), 178.
2. C. Peter Wagner, *How to Have a Healing Ministry Without Making Your Church Sick* (Grand Rapids, MI: Baker Publishing Group, 1988).

Chapter Four

1. M. Scott Peck, *People of the Lie: The Hope for Healing Human Evil* (New York: Simon & Schuster, 1985).
2. Alexsandr Solzhenitsyn, *The Gulag Archipelago Abridged: An Experiment in Literary Investigation*; Thomas P. Whitney, trans. (New York: Harper Perennial, 1985), 75.
3. D. A. Carson. *Showing the Spirit: A Theological Exposition of 1 Corinthians 12–14* (Grand Rapids, MI: Baker Book House 1987), 40.

About the Author

Jeff Kirby serves on the Adult Discipleship Team at The United Methodist Church of the Resurrection. He is a national trainer for the Alpha Course, a national and international educator and speaker, and a consultant on leadership development. His Bible study courses at Resurrection often bring in 500+ participants, who come to hear Jeff's rich and challenging style of teaching.

Jeff is also the co-author of *Journey 101: Knowing, Loving, and Serving God*, published by Abingdon Press.

Journey 101: Knowing God

In *Knowing God*, a six-week study, you will come to know God more fully and discover who you are in God as you gain a better understanding of the essentials of Christian faith.

Journey 101 is a three-part course that guides you on the journey of growing as a Christian. Focusing on core traits of a deeply committed Christian, the series helps you to know, love, and serve God with increasing passion and dedication.

Journey 101 is designed so that everything takes place in the group setting, with no homework outside of class. There is a participant guide and a leader guide for each study, as well as a DVD and a book of daily readings that cover all three studies.

"Journey 101 is a course in the essentials of the Christian life. Participants come away inspired and equipped to know, love, and serve God. It is an important part of Christian discipleship at The Church of the Resurrection!"

—Adam Hamilton, Senior Pastor, The United Methodist Church of the Resurrection

Knowing God Participant Guide 978-1-4267-6574-2
Knowing God Leader Guide 978-1-4267-6575-9
Journey 101 Daily Readings 978-1-4267-6645-9
Journey 101 DVD 978-1-4267-6610-7

Abingdon Press™

Available wherever fine books are sold.

Journey 101: Loving God

In *Loving God*, a six-week study, you will experience spiritual practices that will help you love God and others.

Journey 101 is a three-part course that guides you on the journey of growing as a Christian. Focusing on core traits of a deeply committed Christian, the series helps you to know, love, and serve God with increasing passion and dedication.

Journey 101 is designed so that everything takes place in the group setting, with no homework outside of class. There is a participant guide and a leader guide for each study, as well as a DVD and a book of daily readings that cover all three studies.

"Journey 101 is a course in the essentials of the Christian life. Participants come away inspired and equipped to know, love, and serve God. It is an important part of Christian discipleship at The Church of the Resurrection!"

—Adam Hamilton, Senior Pastor, The United Methodist Church of the Resurrection

Loving God Participant Guide 978-1-4267-6585-8
Loving God Leader Guide 978-1-4267-6583-4
Journey 101 Daily Readings 978-1-4267-6645-9
Journey 101 DVD 978-1-4267-6610-7

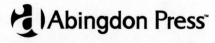
Abingdon Press

Available wherever fine books are sold.

Journey 101: Serving God

In *Serving God*, a six-week study, you will learn how to serve others and, in so doing, share Christ.

Journey 101 is a three-part course that guides you on the journey of growing as a Christian. Focusing on core traits of a deeply committed Christian, the series helps you to know, love, and serve God with increasing passion and dedication.

Journey 101 is designed so that everything takes place in the group setting, with no homework outside of class. There is a participant guide and a leader guide for each study, as well as a DVD and a book of daily readings that cover all three studies.

"Journey 101 is a course in the essentials of the Christian life. Participants come away inspired and equipped to know, love, and serve God. It is an important part of Christian discipleship at The Church of the Resurrection!"

—Adam Hamilton, Senior Pastor, The United Methodist Church of the Resurrection

Serving God Participant Guide 978-1-4267-6586-5
Serving God Leader Guide 978-1-4267-6584-1
Journey 101 Daily Readings 978-1-4267-6645-9
Journey 101 DVD 978-1-4267-6610-7

Available wherever fine books are sold.

CPSIA information can be obtained at www.ICGtesting.com
Printed in the USA
LVOW08s0928100216

474462LV00001B/1/P